Original title:
Roots and Rhymes

Copyright © 2025 Creative Arts Management OÜ
All rights reserved.

Author: Isabella Rosemont
ISBN HARDBACK: 978-1-80567-257-9
ISBN PAPERBACK: 978-1-80567-556-3

Beneath the Old Oak

Under the old oak, squirrels prance,
Chasing their tails, they dance a chance.
Acorns drop, a comical thud,
The ground becomes a nutty flood.

Birds chirp gossip, quite absurd,
Chatting about the latest word.
A wobbly branch plays hide and seek,
As critters giggle, both bold and meek.

Syllables of the Silent

In silence, whispers twist and twirl,
A shy little snail gives a twirl.
Her shell is a house, stylish yet small,
She moves at a pace that's slower than crawl.

A frog cracks jokes, ribbiting loud,
While crickets play tunes, oh so proud.
They sing of the moon and the stars so bright,
Creating a symphony under the night.

Whispers from the Woodlands

Beneath the pines, a fox tells tales,
Of rabbits who wear tiny veils.
Mice in the grass laugh, hiding away,
While deer in the distance, just munch and sway.

A badger dons glasses, reads a book,
While wise old owls just take a look.
Life in the woods is a merry spree,
Where every critter is wild and free.

Stanzas in the Wind

The breeze carries snippets, a fluttering sound,
As dandelions dance round and round.
They giggle and twirl, a soft, gentle ride,
As the wind makes faces, wild and wide.

In the meadow, the flowers do cheer,
For bees come buzzing, oh so near.
They're poets in flight, on a flowery spree,
Writing their verses, just buzzing with glee.

Beneath the Old Oak

Under the oak, the squirrels prance,
Chasing each other, what a dance!
One slips and lands right on his back,
While acorns fall in a clattering pack.

The old tree chuckles, a wise old sage,
As the critters tumble, the scene's all the rage.
Beneath the green canopy, shadows at play,
It's nature's own sitcom, brightening the day.

Nature's Verse

In the garden, the daisies talk,
Swapping tales while butterflies walk.
"Did you see that bee? What a buzz!"
"Yeah, I think he's lost, just like fuzz!"

The daisies laugh, sharing their bloom,
While the sun spills laughter, lighting the room.
A ladybug wobbles, dressed in red,
Stumbling on petals, straight to bed.

Heartstrings of the Past

In the attic, old toys come alive,
A soldier who dreams of a great archive.
He marches around with dust bunnies grand,
While dolls gossip quietly, just as they planned.

A rocking horse hums a forgotten tune,
Recalling adventures under the moon.
The memories dance like shadows in flight,
Bringing giggles to echo through the night.

The Underground Symphony

Down below, where the worms compose,
A symphony plays, in the dirt it grows.
With tiny trumpets and a bass that booms,
They shake the earth in their earthy rooms.

The radishes tap their roots to the beat,
"They've got the moves, can't accept defeat!"
With giggles and grunts, they join the show,
The underground scene, putting on a glow.

A Prayer for the Past

Oh, please let my great-aunt's wig
Not grow wings and start to dance,
I'll hide in the back with a fig,
While she steals the spotlight chance.

Grandpa's stories never fit,
He wrestled bears, but they were pets,
We all pretend to laugh at it,
Yet tell it still with no regrets.

Mom's lasagna's a thick, wild farce,
It might bite back if it could talk,
Each bite, a culinary sparse,
Another toothache on the walk.

So here's to laughter from the past,
The quirks that our family wove,
May they stick around and last,
Like leftovers no one wants to stow.

Harmonies of Heritage

My uncle plays spoons, what a sight,
On Wednesday nights, he can't be stopped,
He jams to the sounds with delight,
While the rest of us cough and flop.

Grandma crochets socks out of thread,
Only for socks that our feet won't fit,
At family gatherings, she said,
Wearing mismatched ones brings the wit.

Cousins gather in a crazy flurry,
They share secrets in a pillow fort,
With giggles and funny, frantic hurry,
Their laughter could surely warp the court.

So let's tune into the funny song,
That echoes through kitchens and halls,
Where memories twist still, all wrong,
And joy flows freely from each of our calls.

The Soil's Serenade

The garden is a place of quirks,
Where the veggies plot to take on life,
Tomatoes in tuxedos do smirks,
While onions conspire to cause strife.

We plant carrots with a poke and shove,
Hoping they'll grow real tall and proud,
But instead it seems, they're in love,
With the cabbage, they're all crowds bowed.

I found a worm with such a grin,
Told me its plans for world domination,
But next to it sat a pickle kin,
And they formed quite the odd tandem station.

So let the earth sing all its tunes,
Of mischief that thrives underground,
In plots of laughter beneath the moons,
Where silly surprises abound.

Roots in the Moonlight

There once was a tree with a hat,
It swayed as the moonlight slipped through,
Squirrels thought it funny and sat,
Making up tales that they knew were true.

Frogs made a choir, loud as frogs can,
Singing of ants that danced with grace,
While fireflies became the lighting plan,
Illuminating this odd little space.

Old branches, they creaked with a chat,
Stories of dirt and the winds that blew,
As crickets joined in just for the pat,
Making the evening feel warm and true.

So here's to the night with a twist,
Where laughter spills out in the glow,
In the shadows, do none resist,
For comedy shines where the moonlight flows.

Voices of the Valley

In the valley, cows make jokes,
They talk of grass and silly hoax.
A chicken danced, a goat just pranced,
Life's a circus; we missed our chance.

The trees are gossiping again,
With leaves that giggle in the rain.
A squirrel claimed he lost his nuts,
While nearby, rabbits laugh in huts.

The river flows with chuckles loud,
As fish swim by and make us proud.
A turtle yelled, "I'm going fast!"
But after that, he fell and crashed.

Oh valley, full of pranks and wit,
With every twist, we can't quite sit.
A place where laughter pokes and prods,
In nature's school, we're all the odds.

In the Garden of Memory

In gardens where old veggies boast,
Tomatoes sing and carrots toast.
The flowers burst with laughter bright,
As bees buzz by in pure delight.

A lettuce leaf confused with grass,
A gnome in trouble on the path.
The daisies wink from side to side,
And grasshoppers join in, oh what a ride!

The sun spills jokes across the ground,
While shadows dance and spin around.
A pumpkin's grinning, what a sight!
In this wild place, all feels just right.

With whispers soft, the memories bloom,
In every corner, joy finds room.
In the garden, laughter blooms divine,
A silly world while sipping thyme.

Silhouettes of Home

In the twilight, shadows play,
A cat's a ninja, or so they say.
The fridge hums tunes, a thief in night,
While socks escape in silly flight.

The couch is where all wisdom lies,
Siblings argue, no one's shy.
A shoe found missing; where's it gone?
The dog, oh wait, it's on his lawn!

Walls remember all the gags,
Like jumping over the old rags.
Faint echoes of laughter fill the air,
As dust bunnies frolic without a care.

Oh silhouettes of life so grand,
In every corner, joy is planned.
Here in the home where whimsy roams,
We find our laughter, our silly poems.

Murmurs of the Meadow

In the meadow, laughter walks,
As crickets sing in tiny talks.
A butterfly with snazzy flair,
Always late, but doesn't care.

The daisies joke of who's the best,
While a bumblebee takes a rest.
The grass does tickle, just for fun,
And even the sun cracks a pun.

A rabbit hops; he trips and rolls,
Fluffy tails and wobbly soles.
The flowers sway to silly tunes,
While parades of ants march under moons.

Murmurs of joy fill the air,
As nature bends without a care.
In this meadow where giggles flow,
Life's a dance we all can show.

Intertwined Legacies

In a garden where time does conspire,
Gnomes wear hats, and squirrels conspire.
Whispers of flowers, a chatty old bunch,
Sharing their secrets, a gossip-filled brunch.

Daisies dance with the wise old oak,
While the sun giggles, and the shadows poke.
Ladybugs strut with a style so unique,
In this circus of life, they play hide and seek.

Seasons of Remembering

Frosty mornings bring hats and hot tea,
While mittens get lost, can't find one or three.
Laughter echoes through snowflakes that fall,
As winter jokingly waits for spring's call.

Then comes the warmth, with blooms all around,
Bees buzzing rhythms, a sweet, buzzing sound.
Naps under the trees hide a wink and a grin,
As children challenge the active catkin.

The Language of Leaves

Whispers in the breeze, oh what a sight,
Leaves argue playfully, who shines the most bright.
Maples chuckle while oaks stand so tall,
In this leafy tableau, it's a free-for-all.

Crisp crunches and rustles, a playful parade,
Nature's own jesters, in sunshine displayed.
Fluttering laughter, how they strategically fall,
A leaf's playful prank, oh, nature's true call.

Threads of Connection

A spider spins tales with silken delight,
While the ants are busy, through day and through night.
Their teamwork is magic, a tiny grand scheme,
In the fabric of life, they all chase a dream.

Mice hold a meeting, all squeaks and all grins,
Sharing the secrets of where the cheese spins.
Families of fungi with jokes up their sleeves,
In this web of connections, everyone weaves.

The Archive of Echoes

In dusty corners, laughter lingers,
With silly tales that twist like fingers.
A shoe tossed high in a lost town hall,
The patchwork quilt that tells it all.

Uncles snagging at their own shoelaces,
Dancing wildly in mismatched braces.
Grandma's secret recipes in a jar,
Finding fun in just who we are.

Weaving the Past

A tapestry of giggles, stitch by stitch,
Knitting yarns where memories twitch.
The cat on the loom thinks it's a ride,
Weaving stories with mischief inside.

The colors clash, a wild parade,
An ancient joke, never to fade.
In every knot, a tale to unfold,
With threads of laughter, bold and gold.

The Heart of the Homeland

In the heart of our land, quirky things play,
Like pigeons that strut in a jazzy ballet.
A road-trip map, with snacks piled high,
Singing off-key as looks pass us by.

The trees might gossip, their leaves all aglow,
While neighbors argue over the best cornbread dough.
Each silly dispute is just part of the game,
And laughter is always the sweetest of fame.

Cadence of the Cosmos

Stars shining bright, a cosmic joke,
Even planets trip on their own bespoke.
Black holes act like they own the dance floor,
While comets chuckle, who wants to explore?

The universe winks, a quirky charade,
In a grand ballet, where light has delayed.
As galactic giggles echo through night,
The cosmos spins on, a laugh in the light.

The Horizon's Embrace

In the far away, the sun does play,
Chasing shadows, making a ballet.
The clouds look like cotton candy spun,
While birds tell jokes, oh what fun!

The sky winks, has secrets untold,
A laugh in the breeze, if you're bold.
It's a circus up there, with no doubt,
Where colors mix and giggles sprout.

The hills wear hats, the trees sport a tie,
While daisies dance, oh my, oh my!
Each sunset brings a comedy show,
Where even the stars put on a glow.

So come laugh with the moon, hum a tune,
As night tickles the sun, inside a cocoon.
The horizon's a stage, wild and free,
A place where life's jokes never flee.

The Loom of Existence

Spinning tales on a cosmic loom,
Threads of laughter sprinkle the room.
Earth's fabric's woven with giggles and glee,
Each moment a stitch, a whimsical spree.

Tangled yarns of hopes and dreams,
Jokes unravel as life brightly beams.
The clowns in the cosmos juggle with flair,
Tickling the stars, a light, silly air.

In the tapestry, colors collide,
Missteps and mishaps, a comical ride.
Frogs in tuxedos leaping with grace,
While time's playful dance takes up its space.

So twirl with the weaver, join in the fun,
As the universe chuckles, we all come undone.
From fibers of joy, let's spin and weave,
For laughter's the thread, in which we believe.

The Portrait of an Epoch

In a gallery filled with curious sights,
Each painting whispers of giggly nights.
Dancing with shadows, the figures prance,
While laughter echoes, inviting a chance.

Each stroke's a jest, a playful delight,
Where moments collide, like day and night.
The canvas chuckles, alive with glee,
As history winks, 'Come dance with me!'

A mustache on a monarch, a crown made of cheese,
The palette of life gets silly with ease.
While silly faces freeze in delight,
Every glance brings laughter, oh what a sight!

So take a step back, enjoy the view,
Each picture tells jokes, some old, some new.
In this epoch's portrait, there's room to play,
For laughter's the color that brightens the day.

Echoes of the Ancestors

In my family tree, there's a parrot,
Cawing secrets from a rusty garret.
A grandpa who danced like a duck,
And a grandma whose jokes ran amok.

A cousin who thinks he's a great chef,
Once burnt down the kitchen—what a jest!
We're all a bit nutty, you might say,
But laughter's the glue that keeps us at play.

Ties Beneath the Surface

Underneath the lawn, there's a tangle,
Of socks and lost toys, oh what a wrangle!
Our history's buried, it seems quite vast,
With mom's shoe collection from years past.

A tree in the yard once sprouted a tire,
We swung until the evening grew dire.
The roots of our antics, they branch and spread,
We're a wild bunch, not easily fed.

Whispers from the Earth

Listen closely! The ground has a tale,
Of gophers who dance when they think they can't fail.
There's a rumor about the worm's hidden stash,
Or at least, a stash for a wriggly bash!

The beetles are laughing, don't take it too hard,
They roll up their snacks like a game of cards.
In this underground circus, we all take a seat,
For every little critter, there's a funny treat.

The Soil's Song

Oh, the soil croons in the morning light,
Of compost tussles and garden delight.
With veggies that giggle and flowers that tease,
The earth sings soft tunes with a cheeky breeze.

As moles wear their shades, looking so cool,
And ladybugs prance like they own the school.
Underneath our feet lies a world full of cheer,
Where laughter and fun are the reasons we're here.

Lyrical Origins

In a garden where words sprout wide,
The old tales tickle, they slide and glide.
Grandma's stories, with giggles she'd share,
Made the past dance like it was still there.

A pun from Dad, with a wink in his eye,
His jokes took flight, like birds in the sky.
Mom rolled her eyes, but chuckled aloud,
In this family, laughter is surely allowed.

Uncles who rhymed, in the silliest ways,
Using voices that echoed through hilarious days.
Their verses were tangled, but so well-defined,
Each line a twist, a fun-loving bind.

So here's to the lines that laugh at their seams,
A merry mix of awkward dreams.
From whimsical words that prance on the page,
To family moments set free from their cage.

Grounded in Memory

Under the porch, tales brewed in a pot,
Spices of laughter, a dash on the spot.
A family tree with branches of cheer,
Growing legends we still hold dear.

There's Uncle Joe, with his mismatched socks,
He strums the banjo and mixes up clocks.
While Auntie Mae, in her garden of puns,
Can turn dirt to fairy tales, all in a run.

The couch becomes a spaceship at night,
As we zoom past the stars in sheer delight.
With pillows as shields, we battle the gloom,
Our laughter breaking the silence of room.

In memory's garden, we plant every jest,
Every chuckle, a staircase towards the best.
Each giggle a root that deepens our ties,
Where whimsy and warmth always rise.

The Dance of Generations

In the living room, shoes flying around,
Grandpa boogies, he's lost and he's found.
Nana's hip sway brings giggles and grins,
Their moves are a show where everyone wins.

Jumping on couches, the kids take the floor,
With disco lights flashing, they're ready for more.
While siblings collide in a rhythmic delight,
Spinning in circles, their futures so bright.

The dog gives a bark as he joins in the fun,
A furry dance partner — oh what a run!
While family photos are taken in haste,
Captured in laughter, no moment to waste.

As generations collide in this whimsical space,
Beneath all the chaos, love we embrace.
With every spin, there's a story that beams,
In this jolly ballet where humor redeems.

Tapestry of Time

Woven with giggles, the fabric of days,
Each thread an echo of childish sways.
Tales that tumble and twist in delight,
Fill each corner of our home with light.

There's mischief in memories, spun by the loom,
A tapestry rich that fills up the room.
From feasts with strange dishes, a delicious mistake,
To pranks that stuck like glue on your cake.

A patch for each sibling, each pet, and each friend,
The laughter entwined, it never does end.
In this patchwork of timing, our stories align,
As we dance through the ages, a grand storyline.

So here's to the scraps that keep us all tied,
With joy in the stitches, we couldn't hide.
In a colorful quilt of quips and delight,
We fashion a world that feels just right.

Ties That Bind

In a garden of oddities, we laugh and play,
While gnomes plot mischief, what a silly display.
With pants that are polka, and hats that are bright,
We'll dance under rainbows, oh what a sight!

Grandpa tells stories of the socks he has lost,
While Auntie insists that her cooking's the boss.
Between spilled lemonade and a pie-shaped scare,
We find family ties in the chaos we share.

A cousin who sings like a crow from a tree,
And uncles who snore like a loud bumblebee.
With humor and hugs we hang tight in this game,
For life's just more fun when we're all a bit lame!

So gather your quirks, your giggles, your quirks,
In the tapestry woven with love and its perks.
With each silly memory, we'll craft our own style,
Ties that bind us together, oh what a wild mile!

Verses from the Earth

Beneath the old oak, where secrets reside,
A worm sings a tune, quite comical in stride.
The daisies debate who's the prettiest bloom,
While frogs croak their dreams from a watery room.

The ants throw a party all under the root,
While butterflies giggle at bugs in a suit.
With laughter and whispers from creatures so small,
We find that the earth holds a story for all.

A scarecrow stands guard with a grin on his face,
While crows snicker softly, protecting their space.
Yet together they bake tiny pies made of dew,
Creating sweet verses of life and its hue.

So join in the games of this whimsical scene,
Where the earth sings its tunes, and all's evergreen.
With laughter and soil, we're free to explore,
In the verses of nature, there's always a score!

Threads of Heritage

In nooks of the attic, the past likes to peek,
With pictures of folks who danced, wore a cheek.
Great-uncle's old sweater, with holes that are grand,
Is now worn by cousin, who just loves the band.

Grandma's recipe book has pages all stuck,
With splatters of sauces, and just plain old luck.
As we feast on the flavors of past, oh so bright,
The laughter erupts like a pie in a fight!

We weave through traditions, each thread tells a tale,
From socks that were knitted to ships set to sail.
A patchwork of memories, oh, what a delight,
In the fabric of life, we sew giggles at night.

So raise up a toast, with lemonade thick,
To the threads that we cherish, the jokes that we pick.
For in every stitch, in each whimsical song,
We find the connection where all of us belong!

Songs of the Soil

In the soil below, where giggles abound,
Earthworms compose symphonies, oh what a sound!
While tumbleweeds tango, the rocks join the fun,
Creating a dance that lasts until the sun.

The daisies wear crowns of the silliest kind,
And the daisies form choirs, all singing aligned.
With laughter in tones, they sway in a breeze,
Making music of memories beneath all the trees.

As kids chase their shadows and crayons run wild,
Their laughter is fresh like the joy of a child.
They dig and they doodle, sketch stories so grand,
In the songs of the soil, there's magic at hand.

So gather your friends, as the sun starts to set,
With nature as witness, we'll create our duet.
For life's just a song, with rhythms to share,
In the melodies sung, there's laughter, and care!

Seeds of Wisdom

In the garden of giggles, we plant our jokes,
With laughter as fertilizer, sprouting pokes.
Each pun a seed that dances in the sun,
We harvest our humor, oh what fun!

Beneath the compost of things gone awry,
We gather our thoughts, let the laughter fly.
Roots stretch deep in the stories we tell,
With quirky anecdotes, we laugh so well.

In the soil of silliness, our dreams take flight,
Sprouting confessions in the dead of night.
We water the puns with true heartfelt cheer,
And watch as each story grows loud and clear.

So plant your jokes, let the laughter grow,
In this whimsical field, there's room for more.
Seeds of absurdity tumble from our minds,
In this madcap garden, true joy you will find!

Legacy in Starlight

Under the moon's grin, we plot our schemes,
With wishes like fireflies, brightening dreams.
Each wink from a star, a wink from the past,
In the night of our tales, we've too much to cast.

Giggles and chuckles make up our fate,
The cosmos exploding, it's never too late.
With comets of laughter orbiting our heads,
We write our own story while laughing in beds.

In the glow of the night, we can't help but smile,
As we journey through space, let's pause for a while.
Our legacy sparkles across the vast sky,
In the laughter we share, our dreams never die.

So dance to the rhythm, the waltz of the stars,
With echoes of giggles from Jupiter to Mars.
The legacy we leave is not written in stone,
But in the quiet giggles that we call our own!

Poignant Petals

In the garden of giggles, blooms start to sway,
With petals of laughter brightening the day.
Each bloom tells a tale, both silly and sweet,
A bouquet of humor, a comedic treat.

With bees that are buzzing, spreading the cheer,
They tickle the blossoms, making fun clear.
The sun shines warmly, as the daisies prance,
In this realm of chuckles, we all take a chance.

A sunflower, grinning, wears shades on its face,
While tulips are twirling in a floral embrace.
In every petal lies a jest tucked away,
Unlocking the giggles in the silliest way.

So smell the sweet laughter, like flowers in bloom,
In this jolly garden, there's always room.
With poignant petals dancing in a fun rhyme,
We celebrate life, one chuckle at a time!

A Chronicle of Shadows

In the shadows of giggles, secrets unfold,
With whispers of joy and stories retold.
Each shadowy figure breaks into a grin,
As the punchlines collide, let the fun begin!

Ghosts wear their smiles, with a wink and a wave,
In this world of jesters, there's no need to save.
The moonlight reveals what we hold back tight,
In the chronicles dark, we burst into light.

With chuckles that echo in corners unseen,
We dance with our fears, lighthearted and keen.
A shadow of silliness creeps up the wall,
In the laughter we share, we conquer it all.

So let's tiptoe through stories, both quirky and bright,
In the chronicle's depth, we find pure delight.
The laughter, a lantern that banishes gloom,
In our balancing act, we all find our room!

Deep Beneath the Grass

In the dirt where the wrigglers dance,
A grandpa worm, he took a chance.
He wore a hat, quite oversized,
And told me jokes that were quite unwise.

The ants all giggled, full of cheer,
As he told tales of yesteryear.
They marched in line without a fuss,
While plotting pranks on that old bus.

A dandelion leaning in near,
Said, "He's the king of this domain here!"
With roots so tangled, yet so spry,
They all agreed, he's the reason why.

Beneath the grass where laughter swells,
Are stories told with earthy smells.
With humor growing, strong and vast,
These silly tales are sure to last.

The Aria of Ancestry

A shout from the tomato, ripe and round,
Said, "In my family tree, I'm so profound!"
With every slice, I share my lore,
Of how I grew on a farmer's floor.

A carrot chimed in, bright and spry,
"I dance in soil, I reach for the sky!"
With leafy greens all boasting their tales,
Of veggie feuds, and giant snails.

The peas jumped in, all in a row,
"We're so united, we steal the show!"
With every pod, there's laughter shared,
In this garden, joy is declared.

From roots to tips, they sing with glee,
A quirky bunch, so wild and free.
An opera sung beneath the sun,
In this veggie realm, all hearts have fun.

Whispers of the Ancients

In the shadows, where the secrets dwell,
A squirrel scolded a tree, oh so swell.
"Why do you stand there, oh great oak?"
"'Cause I grew up here; it's no joke!"

With acorns dropped, the stories fly,
Of reckless winds and the oddest sigh.
A chipmunk chuckled, all ears in tune,
"You're older than dirt, yet never immune!"

A wise old rock added some spice,
"I've seen your drama, once or twice!"
The laughter rang out, through every bough,
Even the roots would giggle somehow.

So listen close to the branches' chat,
For wisdom hides 'neath each fluffy hat.
The whispers echo, light as a breeze,
In nature's court, we laugh with ease.

Echoes Beneath the Surface

Down below where the creatures creep,
A clam boasts tales, oh so deep.
He says he knows where the pearls are found,
In a sea of glee, where joy abounds.

A lobster grinned, pinching with flair,
"I'm the prince of this underwater lair!"
With bubbles rising and laughter shared,
Life in the ocean's never scared.

A starfish chimed, with a voice so meek,
"I've seen it all, just take a peek!"
With arms so wide, they call to play,
In this ocean bed, they roam all day.

From shells to scales, a symphony grows,
In watery depths, where the fun just flows.
So dive right in, and join the cheer,
In echoes below, there's nothing to fear.

Meadows and Monuments

In fields where daisies dance with glee,
A statue sneezes, oh what a spree!
The sun giggles, tickling the grass,
As clouds wear hats, quite the silly class.

Ants march in tune, a minuscule band,
While butterflies join with a wave of their hand.
The brook bubbles laughter, a splashy delight,
As squirrels play hopscotch in humorous flight.

The Void Between Words

In the silence where whispers go,
Lies a joke that steals the show.
A pun like a ninja, swift and sly,
Makes even the grammar rules start to cry.

Letters dance like they've lost their keys,
While commas do cartwheels, if you please.
It's a riddle wrapped up in a grin,
With giggles lurking, it's time to begin!

Timeless Tributes

A clock with hands that shuffle and sway,
Sings of moments that flutter away.
History wears mismatched shoes,
While time trips over its own funny cues.

Echoes of laughter in old tombstone rhymes,
Tickled by giggles of forgotten times.
Each tick a chuckle, each tock a jest,
As past and present waltz at their best.

Sparrows and Secrets

Sparrows gossip with a cheeky flair,
Spreading secrets on the breezy air.
They cackle and chirp as they sip from a cup,
While shadows roll by, trying to keep up.

A cat wearing glasses eavesdrops nearby,
Listening closely with a curious eye.
But the more they squawk, the funnier it gets,
As laughter takes flight with no regrets.

Echoes of the Elders

Old tales dance like a breeze,
Granny's wig sways, oh please!
Uncle Joe lost his left shoe,
And thinks he can still woo.

Auntie's quilt tells secrets low,
Stitched together with a bow.
Cousin Sue sings off the chart,
While Grandpa skips, quick to dart.

Laughter bubbles with every sip,
As Dad acts like he can trip.
Silly stories fill the air,
As shadows wiggle without care.

When we gather, oh what fun!
History shared, jokes overrun.
Echoes of our goofy past,
In our hearts, they forever cast.

Planting Shadows

In the garden, weeds take flight,
Dad insists they're just polite.
Trowels slip and voices cheer,
As we plant snacks right near.

Mom claims that pumpkins are quite rare,
But last year, we grew a bear!
A veggie patch that's quite bizarre,
We've turned it into a snack bazaar.

Sunlight tickles every sprout,
While frogs jump up, singing out!
Our shadows dance on leafy greens,
With giggles hidden in between.

The harvest brings a goofy sight,
Tomatoes dressed as kings in flight!
We eat our treats with joy and glee,
In our quirky family spree.

The Colors of Kinship

A family portrait looks so bright,
Dad in pink, what a sight!
Sister paints with one eye closed,
While the puppy sneezes, oh so posed!

Uncle's hat is on his shoe,
Prices are high for kinship stew!
Auntie laughs, her toes are green,
As the colors blend, a funny scene.

Cousins' pranks keep us on edge,
One steals the last slice of wedge!
With a wink and silly cheer,
We forget laughter's ever near.

Swirling hues and goofy faces,
Family time, the best of places.
In our scrapbook, emotions blend,
An artist's laugh that won't soon end.

Melodies of the Forgotten

A whiskered cat hums a tune,
While Dad clogs to a cracked moon.
Old records spin and laugh along,
As Grandma taps, keeps us strong.

The forgotten tunes return with flair,
While Uncle Jim forgets his chair!
A waltz for a runaway spoon,
As we dance around the living room.

Silly lyrics fill the air,
As Mom belts out a cat's despair.
Grandpa's off-key, but that's just fine,
His snoring's part of the design!

Melodies weave, a frothy scene,
With giggles bursting in between.
In this home where laughter stays,
Music lives in funny ways.

Heritage in Harmony

In the attic, grandma's hats,
Hiding secrets, lots of chats.
A family tree full of quirks,
Where Uncle Joe still does his jerks.

A cousin once tried to bake a pie,
It turned out hard; we wondered why.
We laughed so hard, we almost cried,
While Grandpa snuck a slice and lied.

The stories swirl like wild confetti,
Of long-lost relatives, oh so petty.
We mingle myths, and giggles roam,
In this crazy, loving home.

A family quilt made of odd bits,
Each patch a tale, some real hits.
In harmony, we dance and play,
Our heritage leads the way!

Branching into the Past

My great-aunt's stories give a scream,
Of a cat who stole her ice cream.
In a race, it dashed, oh what a sight,
While she yelled 'Stop!' with all her might.

The family tree's a tangled mess,
With roots that make us all confess.
"Oh, that's Uncle Fred, quite the prank!"
He once put fish in a bank's tank!

Grandma's fingers tap the rhythm,
Of tales that twist, they never dim.
Each branch a laugh, a twist of fate,
In this past, it's never too late.

A treasure hunt of silly ways,
Unfolding tales from pasty days.
With every laugh, we weave a line,
Branching out, and feeling fine!

Beneath the Canopy

Under the shade of a wobbly chair,
A squirrel once spilled mom's dentist chair.
While we all ducked and dodged with flair,
That tale gets told with much despair.

The ceiling fans hum songs from the past,
Of grandma's dance moves that go too fast.
She twirled and spun, oh what a cast,
Her laugh a tune, a spell that lasts.

In the garden, we plant our dreams,
With strawberries bursting at the seams.
Each berry burst brings giggles bright,
As we share stories into the night.

Beneath this canopy, we fill our cup,
With wild tales that just spring up.
Together we laugh until it's late,
With roots that play and orate!

Where Memories Flourish

In a cupboard, past candies and spice,
Lies a photo with Uncle Dice.
Wearing socks that don't match, so bold,
Bringing laughs that never grow old.

At family reunions, the stories unfold,
With grills and games, we're never too cold.
A three-legged race? Oh, what a scene,
When Aunt Lou trips, it's truly keen!

With every bite of cake we share,
Come memories that hang in the air.
These moments bloom, forever bright,
Where laughter lingers into the night.

In the garden of love, we sow our seeds,
And every giggle fulfills our needs.
From silly tales, our joy's nourished,
In a place where laughter's never-finished!

Ties that Bind

In a garden, veggies chat,
Carrots gossip, 'What of that?'
Tomatoes boast of their red hue,
While peas giggle, 'We're hard to chew!'

A cactus claims it's tough and prickly,
But in the rain, it gets quite sickly.
Potatoes hide below the bed,
Laughing at those with sunburned heads.

The flowers dance with a silly sway,
Pretending they don't care what they say.
The sun joins in with a radiant beam,
While the worms wiggle, plotting their scheme.

In this patch, none are shy,
Living life with a wink and a sigh.
Together they twist in a tangled vine,
Savoring jokes like it's all divine!

When Time Weaves

Tick-tock goes the clever clock,
Spinning tales that make us gawk.
Time's a weaver, sly and slick,
Knitting moments with a dip and flick.

Yesterday's socks are lost in the fray,
But they giggle as they lay in dismay.
Tomorrow's shoes are dreaming bold,
Hoping adventure like stories of old.

Ayr no pairs without a mate,
Finding buddies can be fate.
But mismatched ones form a rock band,
Jiving to beats, just as they planned.

So here's to time, our playful muse,
Creating chaos while we snooze.
With every stitch, it crafts a rhyme,
Turning our lives into a fun-time!

The Rhythm of Growth

In a garden where veggies sway,
A radish says, 'I grow each day!'
Lettuce laughs with a leafy grin,
'You sprout so fast, I can't keep in!'

Beets are busy with their red parade,
While mushrooms giggle in the shade.
'Look at us sprout all over the place!
We'll dance till sunset; it's a race!'

The squash, they boast, 'We're big and round!'
While mint pipes in, 'I'm spreading all around!'
But up in the sky, the clouds giggle too,
'Look at those greens; they think they're cool!'

As sunbeams shine on the fragrant patch,
The roots underground begin to hatch.
Amidst the fun, nature spins its charm,
Each sprouting laugh a wholesome balm!

Silent Stories of the Soil

Beneath our feet, the soil teems,
With whispering secrets and funny themes.
Earthworms chuckle as they dig,
'We're just the wriggly folks, that's our gig!'

Ants march in a tiny row,
Sharing tales of seeds that they sow.
'We fought the rain and danced the heat,
The nectar's sweet, it's quite a treat!'

Fungi wink from their shadowy bed,
'We're the goofballs up in your head!'
The roots below tap dance in cheer,
Sending up stories for all to hear.

So when you stroll, just stop and think,
Of all the laughter beneath the brink.
For in the earth, there's joy galore,
With every step, you'll find even more!

Under the Old Sycamore

Beneath the shade, we jig and dance,
The squirrels scurry, in a playful trance.
With acorns falling like tiny bombs,
We dodge and weave, avoiding their charms.

The branches wave as if to cheer,
While birds above croon tunes so clear.
A picnic spread, sandwiches align,
Fingers covered in sticky sweet brine.

Tickling roots, they poke our toes,
A sneaky tickle that nobody knows.
The trunk's old laugh, a creaky sound,
As we play hide and seek around.

We leave a mark on bark, you see,
With heart-shaped carvings and laughter free.
Under the sycamore, we're forever young,
In the shade of stories, our joy is sung.

Reminders from the Ridge

Up on the hill, where the breezes hum,
Lies a cat who thinks he's a drum.
He struts around with a swagger so grand,
While cows nearby just don't understand.

The restless winds whisper old jokes,
That tickle the ears of huddled folks.
Like sheep in coats that don't quite fit,
They laugh and bleat, a comedic skit.

A quirky tree leans, nearly bends,
Holding secrets that never end.
With roots that twist, and bark so rough,
You know it's wise when it's had enough.

From this playful height, the views are clear,
Each chuckle echoing, far and near.
With nature's pranks and playful sights,
We spin our tales on starry nights.

A Symphony of Soil

In gardens where giggles sprout like weeds,
The earth's orchestra plays with fancy leads.
Worms wiggle to a squishy beat,
As daisies tap dance on tiny feet.

The carrots blush, buried deep in brown,
While radishes wear their leafy crown.
On this stage beneath the sun,
The veggies laugh, it's all in fun!

Frogs croak solos from slippery stones,
While crickets chirp in whiny tones.
The plants sway to their growing tune,
With potatoes peeking out, a cheeky boon.

Sprouts and shouts blend in the breeze,
A riot of joy beneath the trees.
In this quirky plot where laughter boils,
We savor the rhythms of happy soils.

The Pulse of the Past

Once lived a tree with tales to tell,
Of squirrels and storms, oh, it knows them well.
With branches wide, it swayed and grinned,
As the sun giggled and the rain skinned.

Old trunks whisper secrets to the breeze,
Of days gone by and silly memories.
A raccoon once wore a hat of leaves,
While bees buzzed tunes that nobody believes.

In the soil, the laughter dwells,
With echoing stories from ancient wells.
From stubborn weeds to daisies grand,
The past comes alive, a playful band.

So here we dance, in nature's place,
Embracing mischief wrapped in grace.
With every step, we feel the beat,
A pulse of joy beneath our feet.

Threads of Identity

In socks of mismatched colors, so bright,
We dance like dandelions, what a sight!
Each thread spun with laughter, nothing's tight,
We wear our quirks like capes, pure delight.

Grandma's stories twist like spaghetti, they twirl,
Of giant cats with hats, oh what a whirl!
With every yarn she spins, our heads unfurl,
With giggles and grins, our hearts all swirl.

A family tree, where the fruit is quite odd,
Each branch a story, each leaf a big nod.
We joke of our quirks, we're a little flawed,
Yet in our mess, we find the joy we've clawed.

So let's stitch together this patchwork parade,
With humor and love, let no charm evade.
In the tapestry of life, we're unafraid,
From funny threads of identity we've made.

Canvases of Memory

With splashes of laughter, we paint the day,
Where colors collide in a silly display.
Our mishaps are brushes that merrily play,
As we canvas our lives in a colorful fray.

A cat with a mustache, what a fine scene,
Or socks on a chicken, such antics obscene!
In each stroke of joy, we create the unseen,
Our memories dance, like a whimsical dream.

The shades of our childhood still brighten our years,
In murals of moments, we laugh through our tears.
In every wild hue, a tale appears,
With giggles and art, we conquer our fears.

So let's mix the palette of happy and bright,
As we color our world in sheer delight.
With canvases bold, we take on the night,
In the gallery of laughter, love takes flight.

Fables from the Forest

In a woodland where giggles grow high as trees,
Bunnies wear slippers and talk with the bees.
A wise old owl tells tales with such ease,
Every fable chips in, like a funny tease.

Squirrels debate on the best acorn pie,
While hedgehogs perform in a tuxedo tie.
Frogs practice ballet, and oh my, how they fly,
With each leap of laughter, our worries say bye!

Through paths filled with jokes, the critters all roam,
In a forest of giggles, we've made our home.
Where shadows share secrets and sunlight will comb,
We weave playful stories, like yarn on a loom.

So join in the frolic, where fun is the quest,
In fables of humor, we each find our jest.
With creatures so quirky, we cheer for the best,
In the heart of this forest, our spirits are blessed.

Where Spirits Whisper

In a land where the giggles hover and dance,
Spirits play hopscotch in a moonlit trance.
They whisper of mischief, and give you a chance,
To join in their fun with a whimsical prance.

One ghost loves donuts, another loves cake,
They argue for hours, for goodness' sake!
While shades in the night play a game of charades,
With laughter as lanterns, our worries they shake.

With chuckles like breezes that sweep through the trees,
These spirits of laughter, they aim to please.
In a swirl of delight, they tease and they squeeze,
Bringing joys from the past with the lightest of keys.

So wander the night where the playful reside,
In whispers of giggles, stay close to their side.
Where fun is the treasure and laughter's the guide,
In the realm of pure glee, let your spirit abide.

Chants of the Forgotten

In the attic where old hats dwell,
A mouse wears one and toasts with shell.
He sings of cheese and a crumbly fate,
While the cat outside sits and awaits.

Old shoes on shelves, they start to dance,
With a rhythm that puts them in a trance.
They kick up dust with every twist,
Swaying gently, they can't resist.

A forgotten broom begins to sweep,
Caught up in laughter, it can't help but leap.
Through cobwebs thick, it twirls about,
In a silly spin, without a doubt.

The lamp flickers, joins in the fun,
Bouncing shadows, they run and run.
In this cluttered house, the joy ignites,
Old things party, the night delights!

Footprints in the Dust

In the garden, a snail is slow,
Leaving trails of glitter and glow.
While the lazy dog rolls in the muck,
Shaking dirt with each goofy cluck.

A squirrel hops with a nut in mouth,
Proclaiming triumph, a royal south.
He slips on leaves, and oh dear me,
His acorn flies like a bumblebee!

The path behind tells tales untold,
Of dancing feet and pranks bold.
Puddles reflect a sky of laugh,
As kids leap in with giggly gaff.

Footprints lead to a treasure hunt,
Where giggles echo, an all-time stunt.
A map made of jelly and candy fine,
For every step, there's a sweet design!

Nurtured by Nature

A tree in the park wears a funky hat,
With leaves like feathers, it looks like that!
Birds perched up sing songs so sweet,
While below, a raccoon tries to dance on his feet.

The flowers gossip, so bright and bold,
About the shy grasshopper, quite old.
He jumps in circles, misses the beat,
While bees buzz by in a dancy retreat.

The sun winks down, a playful tease,
Chasing shadows that sway with the breeze.
The clouds giggle, float high and wide,
As a kite dances, its colors collide.

With each new season, the fun won't cease,
Nature's laughter brings endless peace.
In this garden of giggles and cheer,
Life's playful antics are always near.

A Ballad for the Ages

Once upon a time in a land so small,
A chicken with dreams took a mighty fall.
She strutted and clucked, with an air so grand,
But landed face-first in the mess of the land.

The cow next door with a mooing flair,
Tried to sing, but what a rare affair!
With a hiccup and snort, the barn burst wide,
As laughter erupted on this joyous ride.

The pig in the pen wore a tutu bright,
Twirling and dancing, what a charming sight!
But fell in the mud, turned a glorious shade,
While the rooster laughed loud at the fun they made.

So gather 'round friends for a tale that's true,
Of barnyard antics, just for you.
In the heart of the farm, where the giggles play,
Life is a circus, hip-hip-hooray!

Heartbeats of the Past

In the attic, dust bunnies roam,
Old photos whisper tales of home.
Grandpa's mustache, a laughable sight,
Dancing in the moonlight, oh what a fright!

A wobbly chair tells tales of glee,
As Aunt Edna spills her peach tea.
With every sip, her stories unfold,
Of the time she wore a coat made of gold.

The clock ticks loudly, counting the fun,
Each chime a memory, one by one.
With laughter echoing through the hall,
Let's celebrate those who stood tall!

So here's to the past, let's have a blast,
To each quirky moment that forever will last.
Dancing through history, we chuckle and grin,
For the heartbeat of laughter is where we begin.

Murmurs of the Ancestors

Upon the porch, they gather anew,
Uncles and aunts, a comical view.
With tales so old they've grown some moss,
About a chicken named Super Boss!

Grandma's tales of all her suitors,
Made Dad blush like a bunch of fruiters.
Each story ends with a punchline grand,
As we all clap and give a hand.

Their wisdom wrapped in giggles and fun,
Curly hair like a spun sugar bun.
These whispers dance in the summer air,
As we roll in laughter, a family affair!

So we toast to those who came before,
For every snicker, they open the door.
To a legacy of laughter, tales piled high,
Underneath the starlit sky.

The Hidden Garden

In the backyard grows a treasure chest,
Where carrots wear crowns, who knew they'd jest?
Tomatoes giggle as they turn bright red,
Saying, 'Here comes dinner, hide in your bed!'

A toad hops by, with a top hat askew,
Waving at daisies, they wave back too.
The sunflowers gossip about the bees,
As they sway together in the garden breeze.

A rabbit in glasses reads books on a stump,
While the radishes plot a silvery jump.
In this hidden haven, delight thrives,
With jests and jives that come alive!

So let's dance with the blooms, oh what a scene,
As veggies chuckle, they're never mean.
In nature's laughter, let's all abide,
In this whimsical garden, we'll bide our pride.

Lines of Legacy

A family tree with branches so wide,
Each leaf a giggle, swaying with pride.
Great-great-grandma with her kooky hats,
Started the humor, imagine the chats!

Each letter penned, a jest takes flight,
From the old trunk that squeaks at night.
With ink that dances, they write their woes,
As the parakeet caws and the laughter grows.

In every scrapbook, a treasure trove,
Of failed attempts at romantic love.
Great-uncle Fred in his polka-dot pants,
Captured in time, caught in a trance.

So here's to the laughs that echo with glee,
In the stories we tell, we're wild and free.
Through lines of legacy, fun never dies,
As we share these moments, love multiplies.

Echoing through the Canopy

In the treetops, a squirrel sings,
While a woodpecker dances, tapping things.
Leaves giggle, hiding secrets so sweet,
As a chipmunk shimmies on tiny feet.

A wise old owl cracks a joke,
While a rabbit comes in with a little cloak.
Together they chuckle, a merry band,
Sharing tales of the wild, oh so grand!

Sunlight winks through branches wide,
While vines twist and shout in joy, side by side.
Nature's humor, it never gets old,
With stories of mischief waiting to unfold.

Mushrooms sprout in colorful rows,
Tickling the toes of passing crows.
In this leafy laughter, all is light,
As the day fades softly into the night.

Footfalls in the Forest

There's a rustle in the bushes, a funny sight,
A hedgehog tripped, oh what a flight!
Leaves are laughing, oh can't you see?
Even the branches are shaking with glee.

Amidst the ferns, a tiny frog leaps,
Tickling the nose of a deer that peeps.
The forest floor dances, an amusing show,
As critters parade, in a wild, funny flow.

Ants march in sync, clumsy parade,
While butterflies giggle, oh how they're swayed!
What a ruckus, what a fun spree,
In this enchanted wood, all are carefree.

With every footfall, a tale unwinds,
Nature's slapstick, where joy is confined.
Follow the laughter, it's easy to find,
In the whims of the wild, we're all entwined.

Choruses of Connection

In the morning light, the frogs croak a tune,
While raccoons in masks dance under the moon.
With notes of the breeze, they craft a song,
Even the grumpy old bear hums along!

The flowers sway, a giggling crowd,
As the wind tells tales, lively and loud.
Each note a wink, a chuckle, a cheer,
In every harmony, laughter draws near.

The bees buzz in rhythm, a comic parade,
Tickling petals, in joyous cascade.
The trees sway with laughter, leaves turning bright,
Creating a symphony of pure delight.

As the day fades to the colors of night,
Crickets join in, making everything right.
This jolly orchestra never will cease,
In the whispers of nature, we find our peace.

Tides of Tradition

Once a year, the llamas convene,
In a silly old hat, a sign of the scene.
With a twirl and a twirl, they frolic around,
Making a splash in laughter unbound.

The turtles tiptoe, a comical sight,
As they strut their stuff in the golden sunlight.
With shells that shine and personalities too,
Each one has a story, oh, who knew?

Fish swim by with a giggling splash,
As the swings on the branches make a dash.
Nature's tradition, a fun-loving spree,
Where every little critter joins the jubilee.

As the moon rises, the laughter takes flight,
With fireflies glowing, creating the light.
In the tides of the wild, a gathering so grand,
A funny little circus, all hand in hand.

The Archive of Autumn

Leaves fall like laughter, soft and round,
Each twist and tumble, joy profound.
Squirrels stash treasures, nuts galore,
While I trip on acorns, begging for more.

Pumpkins grin wide, in the patch they bake,
As ghosts pull pranks, for goodness sake!
Cider flows sweet, spiced and bright,
Who needs a costume? I'm high on the bite!

Scarves fly like flags in gusty weather,
While I chase my hat, oh, what a tether!
The harvest moon winks, a cheeky tease,
As I dance with shadows, done with ease.

So gather 'round for laughter's delight,
In the archive of autumn, joy takes flight.
With every chuckle, the season's best,
Ripened with giggles, we leave the rest.

Metaphors of the Mountain

Up high in the mountains, wisdom grows,
With every step, a tale that flows.
Boulders grin wide, like old pals at play,
While I stumble on trails, come what may.

The breeze whispers secrets, oh how it teases,
In the trees, squirrels hoard winter's cheeses.
Climbing up high, I engage in a race,
The summit awaits, but I'm lost in a case!

Avalanches chuckle, as I seek my way,
Mischievous rocks give life a funny play.
My hiking boots squeak like a kid's rubber toy,
Each laugh echoes back, with mountain joy.

So let's toast to peaks and missteps galore,
Where humor abounds, and spirits explore.
For laughter is king, and adventure's our rhyme,
In the metaphors crafted by nature and time.

A Pathway of Imprints

Footprints scattered, like breadcrumbs of cheer,
Each step a giggle, as I tiptoe near.
The path of my life, a wonky line,
With scribbles of dreams, oh how they shine!

Mud pies and puddles, splashes of fun,
An adventure awaits, out under the sun.
Bicycles wobble, like clumsy old friends,
And laughter erupts, as the mayhem descends.

The garden's a canvas, with weeds that perform,
They dance like mad hatters, in a jumbled swarm.
With carrots like trumpets, they blare out their tune,
While I trample through laughter, like a silly cartoon.

So let's skip together, on this quirky trail,
With giggles and petals, we'll never derail.
For every imprint tells a tale that's sublime,
In the pathway of joy, we create our own climb.

Verses Woven in Time

Threads of laughter stitch the days,
With every stitch, a funny phrase.
Fiber-optic humor, woven tight,
Glowing in the dark, oh what a sight!

The fabric of stories, colors collide,
While clumsy hands fumble with pride.
With a needle of joy, thoughts take flight,
Making mischief under the moonlight.

Some knots are tangled, with puns intertwined,
Clotheslines of giggles, whimsically designed.
An outfit of memories, joyful and bright,
Wrapped in the fabric of pure delight.

So let's dance through the seams, unravel our plots,
In this tapestry woven, there's laughter, no spots.
For in each little stitch, our spirits climb high,
In the verses of life, we just can't deny.

Echoes of the Hearth

In a nook where shadows play,
Grandpa's tales lead us astray.
He swears the stew stirs itself,
While dancing beans hide on the shelf.

A pot that bubbles, sings with glee,
Whispers of laughter and spilled tea.
As socks on the line take a kite's flight,
We giggle at socks, what a sight!

A cat that thinks he holds the throne,
Rules the roost, and steals the bone.
With each pat, the dog rolls his eyes,
While a feather duster plots its surprise.

As the fire crackles with furry cheer,
Even the chairs lend us their ear.
In this space, joy's license is free,
Life's

a sitcom, come sit with me!

Deep Waters

Down by the creek where the frogs like to prance,
Silly fish put on a splashy dance.
They wiggle and squirm with stylish flair,
While turtles just grumble from their comfy lair.

The ducks wear hats that float on their heads,
Quacking in sync as they play with the threads.
If fish could laugh, oh what a show,
As they tease the catfish with tales we don't know.

A canoe drifts by with a squirrel at the helm,
He tips a nut like he's running a realm.
The beavers work hard, they build with a grin,
Who knew that wood was their ultimate win?

In the babbling brook where stories collide,
Fish and fowl and friends take a ride.
Every ripple a joke, every splash a delight,
In these deep waters, life's truly just right!

Strong Currents

The river laughed with a mighty roar,
It tickled the banks, 'Come paddle some more!'
The canoes wobbled like a puppy on ice,
While splashes broke out with laughter so nice.

Fish fashioned hats with a playful twist,
Casting nets made of dreams, none to be missed.
They cheered for the sun with a shimmering glance,
'Let's dance on the waves, let's give it a chance!'

The wind sang songs, pulling every face,
As the turtles slid by at a leisurely pace.
A squirrel did cartwheels, oh what a view!
While the frog claimed the crown—he won with a cue.

In the swirl of the stream, we giggled and spun,
Making memories here under the sun.
With so much to share, the current's our guide,
Let's ride out the rapids, side by side!

Beneath the Canopy

Beneath the leaves where shadows leap,
The forest whispers secrets we keep.
A squirrel insists on telling a joke,
While the rabbits all nod, don't underestimate folk.

The trees wear crowns made of glittering light,
Where fireflies flicker as day turns to night.
A wise old owl hoots with delight,
'Can you hear the rhythm? It's music tonight!'

With branches as arms that stretch far and wide,
The roots may be tangled, but we're the wild ride.
In the ferns and the fables, we laugh and we sway,
Under the canopy, we dance and we play.

With every rustle, stories unfold,
In this enchanted place, funny tales never get old.
Join the critters, let the giggles ignite,
Beneath the canopy, everything's right!

The Language of the Land

The hills hold a giggle within every creak,
With valleys that chuckle, they're never meek.
Mountains draped in fuzzy green coats,
Take selfies with clouds and erupt colorful notes.

Rivers gossip, bubbling with cheer,
Pond frogs croak like they're at a frontier.
The daisies sass with their bright little heads,
'Why hurry through life, just heed what we said!'

With whispering winds that tickle the trees,
Nature herself speaks softly with ease.
An orchestra plays, but the humor is grand,
For laughter and joy, are the tools of the land.

In every nook, the earth has a grin,
Join in the fun and let's all spin.
With sunbeams and shadows, come take a stand,
In the language of life, let's form a band!

From Seed to Stanza

In a garden plot where giggles sprout,
Tiny veggies dance, there's no doubt.
Carrots wear glasses, and peas wear hats,
Swapping their stories like chattering bats.

A radish proclaims, 'I'm quite the chef!'
While corn's in the kitchen, cooking up theft.
Tomatoes roll dice, all laughs in the air,
As laughter germinates everywhere!

With each little seed, a tale to unfold,
Funny adventures in soil so bold.
What grows in our hearts? A humor divine,
Dig deep and you'll find every giggle's a sign.

So water those dreams with a sprinkle of cheer,
Laughter's the fertilizer, that much is clear.
From tiny beginnings, fun tales will arise,
Just watch as they flourish, a joy to the eyes.

The Tapestry of Tradition

In a house that's filled with stories retold,
Grandma's old quilt, with patches of gold.
Each stitch is a memory, wrinkled and bright,
Like squirrels in pajamas, it's quite a sight!

Uncles tell jokes that are older than time,
While Auntie crochets a hat that won't rhyme.
Family feuds break over pie and some cake,
Nothing like laughter to make the hearts quake!

Dancing in circles, the old tune's a groan,
Yet everyone laughs, no one's left alone.
A trumpet's a puppy, a banjo's a cat,
In this quirky tradition, there's rhythm to that!

Oh, the lessons we learn from the quirks in our clan,
From of tales of a fisherman and all that he ran.
So gather 'round close, leave your worries inside,
In a tapestry woven where silliness hides.

Gnarled Tales of Yore

Beneath the old oak with branches like arms,
Sit the wise old gnomes swapping silly charms.
With hats that are crooked, and noses that glow,
They tell me of mischief from long, long ago.

One gnome rode a snail, the other grew wings,
Claiming all trees had the most peculiar things.
They debated the weather and fables of fright,
While squirrels kept score of their droll little fight.

Creaking and cracking, the old tree stood by,
Listening to laughter as clouds drifted high.
Gnarled tales of the past, all twisted and fun,
Each story a breeze, warm under the sun.

So gather 'round tightly, let their stories tease,
Of pumpkin relays and snappy old bees.
In shadows of laughter, a joy to explore,
There's nothing quite like those gnarled tales of yore.

Inherit the Melody

In a bustling kitchen where chaos ignites,
The pots play the symphony, much to their delight.
Spatulas clatter, and pans start to dance,
As the clock chimes the rhythm, they all join in prance.

A salad sings loudly, a chorus of greens,
While cookies are whispering sweet little dreams.
The fridge hums a tune, with a sprinkle of spice,
Making music together, oh isn't that nice?

Uncle Sam's trumpet lets out a loud honk,
While Aunt Bet's blender just rumbles and clonk.
With laughter and madness, it's a dish that's divine,
Each bite a new rhyming, a joy so benign.

So take a big scoop of this family feast,
And share all the melodies, laughter released.
For in every tune, and each joyful decree,
We inherit the music of family glee.

www.ingramcontent.com/pod-product-compliance
Lightning Source LLC
Chambersburg PA
CBHW051645160426
43209CB00004B/796